A Mirror to the Soul

Thirty Contemporary Hymns
based on the Psalms

TIMOTHY DUDLEY-SMITH

music editor:

WILLIAM LLEWELLYN

Published in the UK in 2013 by
The Royal School of Church Music
19 The Close, Salisbury, Wilts, SP1 2EB
Tel: +44 (0)1722 424848   Fax: +44 (0)1722 424849
E-mail: press@rscm.com Website: www.rscm.com
Registered charity 312828

Also by the same author:
Beneath a travelling Star: thirty contemporary carols and hymns for Christmas
A Calendar of Praise: thirty contemporary hymns for seasons of the Christian Year
High Days and Holy Days: thirty contemporary hymns for annual occasions
in the life of the local church
The Voice of Faith: thirty contemporary hymns for Saints' Days
or based on the liturgy
Above Every Name: thirty contemporary hymns in praise of Christ
Draw Near to God: thirty contemporary hymns for worship, mainly for the pastoral Services

Cover design by Anthony Marks
Music Engraving by William Llewellyn, Devon, UK
Typesetting and layout by RSCM PRESS
Printed in England by Halstan & Co, Amersham

PREFACE

Psalms gave the Christian community its first hymns. Indeed, the Hebrew name for our Book of Psalms means 'Songs of Praise'.

Because psalms speak not only of God as active in history, and of his universal majestic creative power, but as a God known in personal encounter, and open to every cry of the human heart, the book has been, for more than a thousand years, what Calvin described as a 'glass' or mirror:

> "… for not an affection will a man find in himself, an image of which is not reflected in this glass. Nay, all the griefs, sorrows, fears, misgivings, hopes, cares, anxieties, in short, all the troublesome emotions with which the minds of men are wont to be agitated, the Holy Spirit has here pictured to the life."

Even in many Anglican churches today, the chanting of psalms is becoming a lost art. Metrical psalms are not, except in the rarest cases, actual translations of the original, but to congregations used to hymn singing they can offer something of the riches that singing (or saying) of the psalms provide.

As with those metrical psalms in regular use (*The King of love my shepherd is; Through all the changing scenes of life; O God, our help in ages past* to name a few examples) the hymns in this collection claim no more than to be 'based on' the psalm in question; and of course, as with the examples above, they can be sung in their own right as hymns, regardless of their origin.

A glance at themes represented (following the first line, on the Contents page) will show the kind of variety that will often fit easily into a pattern of worship; or be of help in private devotion.

Timothy Dudley-Smith
November 2013
Ford, Salisbury

CONTENTS

1 How happy those who walk in truth

GREAT WALDINGFIELD

86 88 86

1. How hap-py those who walk in truth, nor make the wrong their choice, nor take the path that sin-ners tread, nor sit where scorn-ful words are said, but in the law of God are led to won-der and re-joice.

Music: ROBIN WELLS (*b.* 1943)

PSALM 1

Christian experience and discipleship

How happy those who walk in truth,
    nor make the wrong their choice,
nor take the path that sinners tread,
nor sit where scornful words are said,
but in the law of God are led
    to wonder and rejoice.

2   The meditations of their heart
        by day and night incline
to ponder God's eternal word
and find, with soul and conscience stirred,
the very voice of God is heard,
    a law of life divine.

3   As trees beside the water stand
        in summer's splendour seen,
and nourished by the streams that flow
their ripened fruits in season show,
so shall the godly thrive and grow,
    whose leaves are always green.

4   The wicked fly like scattered chaff
        upon the wind away:
the Lord shall drive them forth as dust,
but those who in his mercy trust
await the mansions of the just
    in everlasting day.

Alternative tunes: REVELATION *or* WITHINGTON

2 i How great our God's majestic Name!

SONG 34 (ANGELS' SONG)   LM

1. How great our God's ma-jest-ic Name! His glo-ry fills the earth and sky. His praise the_ heaven-ly host_ pro-claim,____ e-ter-nal God_ and Lord most_ high.

Music: Melody and bass by
ORLANDO GIBBONS (1583–1625)

PSALM 8

Praise to the Creator

How great our God's majestic Name!
    His glory fills the earth and sky.
His praise the heavenly host proclaim,
    eternal God and Lord most high.

2   His fingers set the moon in place,
        the stars their Maker's hand declare;
in earth and sky alike we trace
        the pattern of his constant care.

3   And what of us? Creation's crown,
        upheld in God's eternal mind;
on whom he looks in mercy down
        for tender love of humankind.

4   His praise the heavenly host proclaim
        and we his children tell his worth:
how great is God's majestic Name,
        his glory seen in all the earth!

2 ii How great our God's majestic Name!

NIAGARA

LM

1. How great our God's ma - jest - ic Name! His glo - ry fills the earth and sky. His praise the heaven - ly host pro - -claim, e - ter - nal God and Lord most high.

Music: ROBERT JACKSON (1840–1914)

PSALM 8

Praise to the Creator

How great our God's majestic Name!
  His glory fills the earth and sky.
His praise the heavenly host proclaim,
  eternal God and Lord most high.

2 His fingers set the moon in place,
  the stars their Maker's hand declare;
in earth and sky alike we trace
  the pattern of his constant care.

3 And what of us? Creation's crown,
  upheld in God's eternal mind;
on whom he looks in mercy down
  for tender love of humankind.

4 His praise the heavenly host proclaim
  and we his children tell his worth:
how great is God's majestic Name,
  his glory seen in all the earth!

Alternative tune: DUKE STREET

3 Lord, when the storms of life arise

CLOTH FAIR   86 88 6

Lyrics beneath the music:

1. Lord, when the storms of life arise be near to keep me yet, my cho-sen por-tion and my prize in whom a-lone my re-fuge lies, on whom my hope is set.

Music: JOHN SCOTT (*b.* 1956)

Psalm 16

God our strength and refuge; pilgrimage

Lord, when the storms of life arise
    be near to keep me yet,
my chosen portion and my prize
in whom alone my refuge lies,
    on whom my hope is set.

2   In God alone securely stand
    his saints for ever blest,
who shelter safe beneath his hand
as in a fair and pleasant land,
    and in his presence rest.

3   Lord of our life, our strength and stay,
    whom yet unseen we love,
uphold us in the narrow way
and guide our footsteps night and day
    with wisdom from above.

4   So shall the path of life be shown,
    the prayers of faith ascend;
until we know as we are known,
and sing before the Father's throne
    the songs that never end.

Alternative tune: REPTON

4 The stars declare his glory

GIBSON

76 86 86

1. The stars de-clare his glo - ry; the vault of hea-ven springs___

mute wit-ness of__ the Mas-ter's hand in__ all cre-at-ed things,___

and through the si - lenc - es of space their sound-less mu - sic sings.

Music: PATRICK WEDD (*b.*1948)

PSALM 19

Creation; Scripture; providence

THE STARS declare his glory;
    the vault of heaven springs
mute witness of the Master's hand
    in all created things,
and through the silences of space
    their soundless music sings.

2   The dawn returns in splendour,
      the heavens burn and blaze,
the rising sun renews the race
    that measures all our days,
and writes in fire across the skies
    God's majesty and praise.

3   So shine the Lord's commandments
      to make the simple wise;
more sweet than honey to the taste,
    more rich than any prize,
a law of love within our hearts,
    a light before our eyes.

4   So order too this life of mine,
      direct it all my days;
the meditations of my heart
    be innocence and praise,
my Rock, and my redeeming Lord,
    in all my words and ways.

5 The Lord be near us as we pray

ARLETTE

888 6 D

1. The Lord be near us as we pray and help us, through the darkest day, to find our spirits' strength and stay in his most holy Name. To him be heartfelt homage paid and sacrifice of prayer be made; in him we trust, and undismayed his promised presence claim.

Music: RONALD TURNER (*b.*1946)

PSALM 20

Trusting God's faithfulness

THE LORD be near us as we pray
and help us, through the darkest day,
to find our spirits' strength and stay
 in his most holy Name.
To him be heartfelt homage paid
and sacrifice of prayer be made;
in him we trust, and undismayed
 his promised presence claim.

2 May God our dearest hopes fulfil
and move our hearts to seek his will,
rejoicing in his triumph still
 and his prevailing Name;
who hears and answers all our prayers,
who knows the weight of human cares,
and in his Son our nature shares,
 for evermore the same.

3 Let others trust in wealth and power
to save them in the evil hour,
we find our refuge and our tower
 in God's eternal Name;
in him to stand, secure and strong,
believers who to Christ belong,
and with his saints in ceaseless song
 his faithfulness proclaim.

Alternative tune: BROOKSHILL

6 We sing the Lord our light

WATLINGTON HILL

66 66 44 44

Unison

1. We sing the Lord our light; our strength, who walk his
4. His love will still pre - vail, his might - y hand up -

way; though full of fears the night, though long and
hold, though kith and kin may fail and dear - est

hard the day. His mer - cy kind we
hearts grow cold; be pa - tient yet! his

bold - ly claim who in his Name sal - va - tion find.
king - dom own, in whom a - lone our hopes are set!

Music: JOHN BARNARD (*b.*1948)

Psalm 27

God's strength, grace and love

Optional compatible harmony version for verses 2 & 3

2. To him we make re - quest;____ this prayer a - lone we
3. In trou - ble's dark - est day____ his strength is near at

bring:____ that in his pre - sence blest we may be -
hand;____ in dan - ger or dis - may up - on his

hold____ our King;____ by his free grace dis -
rock____ we stand.____ O an - xious heart, for -

cern his will, and wor - ship still be - fore____ his____ face.
sake your fear for God is here to take____ your____ part!

7 Happy are those, beyond all measure blessed

ARGIANO

10 10 10 10 10 10

Buoyant yet steady

Unison

1. Hap - py are those,_____ be- -yond all mea-sure blessed,_____ who know their guilt is gone, their faults for - given; who taste the joys_ that come from sin_____ con-fessed, whose hearts are blame-less in the sight_ of heaven. Bless-ings are ours be-neath a Fa - ther's hand; by love made wel - come,

Music: WILLIAM LLEWELLYN (*b.*1925)

PSALM 32

Forgiveness; security; guidance

HAPPY are those, beyond all measure blessed,
    who know their guilt is gone, their faults forgiven;
who taste the joys that come from sin confessed,
    whose hearts are blameless in the sight of heaven.
        Blessings are ours beneath a Father's hand;
        by love made welcome, uncondemned we stand.

2   God is our strength when troubles flood the heart;
    from his high throne he stoops to hear our prayer.
When trials come, the Lord shall take our part,
    our Rock of refuge from the storms of care.
        Safely enfolded in his keeping strong,
        his sure salvation is our triumph-song.

3   God is our guide who watches all our way;
    gently he teaches us our path to find.
Be not self-willed, like beasts that go astray,
    God will direct our feet and form our mind:
        mercy embraces us on every side
        with God our joy, our Saviour, strength and guide.

8 Tell his praise in song and story

ABBOT'S LEIGH

87 87 D

1. Tell his praise in song and sto-ry, bless the Lord with
heart and voice; in my God is all my glo-ry, come be-
-fore him and re-joice. Join to praise his Name to-geth-er,
he who hears his peo-ple's cry; tell his praise, come
wind or wea-ther, shin-ing fac-es lift-ed high.

Music: CYRIL VINCENT TAYLOR (1907–1991)

PSALM 34

Experience; testimony; praise

TELL his praise in song and story,
    bless the Lord with heart and voice;
in my God is all my glory,
    come before him and rejoice.
Join to praise his Name together,
    he who hears his people's cry;
tell his praise, come wind or weather,
    shining faces lifted high.

2   To the Lord whose love has found them
    cry the poor in their distress;
swift his angels camped around them
    prove him sure to save and bless.
God it is who hears our crying
    though the spark of faith be dim;
taste and see! beyond denying
    blest are those who trust in him.

3   Taste and see! In faith draw near him,
    trust the Lord with all your powers;
seek and serve him, love and fear him,
    life and all its joys are ours:
true delight in holy living,
    peace and plenty, length of days;
come, my children, with thanksgiving
    bless the Lord in songs of praise.

4   In our need he walks beside us,
    ears alert to every cry;
watchful eyes to guard and guide us,
    love that whispers 'It is I.'
Good shall triumph, wrong be righted,
    God has pledged his promised word;
so with ransomed saints united
    join to praise our living Lord!

Alternative tune: HYFRYDOL (No.23 in this book)

9 i Lord, may our hearts within us burn

ABINGDON

88 88 88

1. Lord, may our hearts within us burn and grant us grace to inter-cede, to know compassion and concern for those in every kind of need, whose lives are seen as little worth, the poor and helpless of the earth.

Music: ERIK ROUTLEY (1917–1982)

PSALM 41

Compassion; trust and confidence

LORD, may our hearts within us burn
    and grant us grace to intercede,
to know compassion and concern
    for those in every kind of need,
        whose lives are seen as little worth,
        the poor and helpless of the earth.

2   In God alone his people stand,
    he keeps us in the evil day,
our lives are lived beneath his hand,
    his blessings lie about our way:
        in sin or sickness, hear our plea,
        'O Lord, be merciful to me.'

3   And when my days on earth shall end,
    should foes unite against my name,
or should my own familiar friend
    our lifelong bond of love disclaim,
        should hope decline and courage flee,
        O Lord, be merciful to me.

4   Our God shall not forsake his own,
    stronger than death his boundless grace.
When with the saints about his throne
    pardoned we stand before his face,
        'Glory to God', our song be then,
        'Glory to God, Amen, Amen.'

9 ii Lord, may our hearts within us burn

ST CATHERINE

88 88 88

1. Lord, may our hearts within us burn and grant us grace to inter-cede, to know compassion and concern for those in every kind of need, whose lives are seen as little worth, the poor and helpless of the earth.

Music: HENRI FRIEDRICH HEMY (1818–1888)
adapted by JAMES GEORGE WALTON (1821–1905)

PSALM 41

Compassion; trust and confidence

LORD, may our hearts within us burn
    and grant us grace to intercede,
to know compassion and concern
    for those in every kind of need,
        whose lives are seen as little worth,
        the poor and helpless of the earth.

2   In God alone his people stand,
        he keeps us in the evil day,
our lives are lived beneath his hand,
    his blessings lie about our way:
        in sin or sickness, hear our plea,
        'O Lord, be merciful to me.'

3   And when my days on earth shall end,
        should foes unite against my name,
or should my own familiar friend
    our lifelong bond of love disclaim,
        should hope decline and courage flee,
        O Lord, be merciful to me.

4   Our God shall not forsake his own,
        stronger than death his boundless grace.
When with the saints about his throne
    pardoned we stand before his face,
        'Glory to God', our song be then,
        'Glory to God, Amen, Amen.'

10 God is my great desire

LEONI

66 84 D

1. God is my great de - sire, his face I seek the first;
to__ him my heart and soul as-pire, for him I__ thirst.
As__ one in de-sert lands, whose ve - ry__ flesh__ is flame,__
in burn-ing love I__ lift my__ hands and__ bless his__ Name.

Music: Hebrew melody
    notated by THOMAS OLIVERS (1725–1799)

Psalm 63

Thirst for God; hope and joy

God is my great desire,
    his face I seek the first;
to him my heart and soul aspire,
    for him I thirst.
As one in desert lands,
    whose very flesh is flame,
in burning love I lift my hands
    and bless his Name.

2   God is my true delight,
    my richest feast his praise,
through silent watches of the night,
    through all my days.
To him my spirit clings,
    on him my soul is cast;
beneath the shadow of his wings
    he holds me fast.

3   God is my strong defence
    in every evil hour;
in him I face with confidence
    the tempter's power.
I trust his mercy sure,
    with truth and triumph crowned:
my hope and joy for evermore
    in him are found.

11 A King on high is reigning

WOLVERCOTE

76 76 D

1. A King on high is reign-ing whom end-less a-ges bless, from sea to sea sus-tain-ing his rule of right-eous-ness. Be-neath his strong de-fend-ing his peo-ple stand se-cure, whose just-ice knows no end-ing while sun and moon en-dure.

Music: WILLIAM HAROLD FERGUSON (1874–1950)

PSALM 72

'The sovereign Lord of all'

A KING on high is reigning
   whom endless ages bless,
from sea to sea sustaining
   his rule of righteousness.
Beneath his strong defending
   his people stand secure,
whose justice knows no ending
   while sun and moon endure.

2   As rains that gently nourish
   and bring the seed to birth,
his righteousness shall flourish,
   his peace possess the earth;
her sceptred kings acclaim him,
   before his feet they fall,
the nations kneel to name him
   the sovereign Lord of all.

3   The poor are in his keeping,
   he hears their bitter cry,
his watchfulness unsleeping
   to answer every sigh;
the lonely and neglected,
   the outcast and in need,
forsaken and rejected,
   to him are dear indeed.

4   His Name endures for ever
   who formed the fertile land;
the fruits of our endeavour
   shall prosper in his hand.
With prayer and song and story
   his praises sound again,
in all the earth his glory;
   so be it, Lord! Amen!

Alternative tune: KING'S LYNN (No.28 in this book)

12 For God my spirit longs

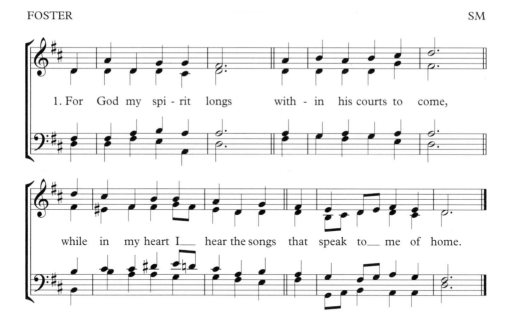

1. For God my spi-rit longs with-in his courts to come,

while in my heart I___ hear the songs that speak to__ me of home.

Music: MYLES BIRKET FOSTER (1851-1922)

PSALM 84

God our eternal home

FOR GOD my spirit longs
    within his courts to come,
while in my heart I hear the songs
    that speak to me of home.

2   The sparrow builds her nest,
        the swallow lays her young:
    may my long home be with the blest
        who hear God's praises sung.

3   My journey be with those
        whose pilgrim feet have trod
    where water in the desert flows,
        a highway home to God.

4   To him, when life is past,
        my song shall still be praise;
    our Sun and Shield while time shall last,
        and to eternal days.

Optional alternative harmonization for verse 4

Choir and Organ.
Congregation sing melody opposite.

Version from
The Clarendon Hymn Book 1936

4. To him, when life is past, my song shall still be praise;

our Sun and Shield while time shall last,__ and to__ e - ter - nal days.

Alternative tune: CARLISLE

13 i Timeless love! We sing the story

BODAFON FIELDS

87 87 77

Unison

1. Time - less love! We sing the sto - ry, praise his won-ders, tell his
worth; love more fair than hea-ven's glo - ry, love more
firm than an-cient earth! Tell his faith-ful-ness a - broad:

Choir descant (small notes)

who is like him? Praise_____ the Lord!

PSALM 89. 1–8

God as loving, just and faithful

TIMELESS LOVE! We sing the story,
praise his wonders, tell his worth;
love more fair than heaven's glory,
love more firm than ancient earth!
    Tell his faithfulness abroad:
    who is like him? Praise the Lord!

2   By his faithfulness surrounded,
north and south his hand proclaim;
earth and heaven formed and founded,
skies and seas, declare his Name!
    Wind and storm obey his word:
    who is like him? Praise the Lord!

3   Truth and righteousness enthrone him,
just and equal are his ways;
more than happy, those who own him,
more than joy, their songs of praise!
    Sun and Shield and great Reward:
    who is like him? Praise the Lord!

Music: WILLIAM LLEWELLYN (*b.*1925)

13 ii Timeless love! We sing the story

PATRIXBOURNE

87 87 77

1. Time - less love! we sing the sto - ry, praise his won - ders, tell his worth; love more fair than hea - ven's glo - ry, love more firm than an - cient earth! Tell his faith - ful - ness a - broad: who is like him? Praise the Lord!

Music: JOHN BARNARD (*b.*1948)

Psalm 89. 1–8

God as loving, just and faithful

Timeless love! We sing the story,
praise his wonders, tell his worth;
love more fair than heaven's glory,
love more firm than ancient earth!
    Tell his faithfulness abroad:
    who is like him? Praise the Lord!

2   By his faithfulness surrounded,
north and south his hand proclaim;
earth and heaven formed and founded,
skies and seas, declare his Name!
    Wind and storm obey his word:
    who is like him? Praise the Lord!

3   Truth and righteousness enthrone him,
just and equal are his ways;
more than happy, those who own him,
more than joy, their songs of praise!
    Sun and Shield and great Reward:
    who is like him? Praise the Lord!

Alternative tune: TIMELESS LOVE

14 Angelic hosts above

HAREWOOD

66 66 44 44

1. Angelic hosts above the Lord of glory praise, his faithfulness and love from everlasting days. His Name declare in earth and sky! With God Most High who can compare?

Music: SAMUEL SEBASTIAN WESLEY (1810–1876)

PSALM 89. 5–18

God Most High; in creation, faithfulness and love

ANGELIC hosts above
    the Lord of glory praise,
his faithfulness and love
    from everlasting days.
      His Name declare
        in earth and sky!
      With God Most High
        who can compare?

2   How awesome his decrees,
    his mighty hand displayed!
He calms the raging seas
    and rules the worlds he made.
      From nature's night
        he brought to birth
      the founded earth,
        the starry height.

3   Before his judgment seat,
    where justice rules alone,
his truth and mercy meet,
    the pillars of his throne.
      Supreme he reigns,
        who by his power
      from hour to hour
        the world sustains.

4   Secure beneath his care
    rejoice to walk his way,
and in his presence share
    the light of heaven's day.
      His Name adored,
        to faith revealed,
      is King and Shield
        and glorious Lord!

Alternative tune: DARWALL'S 148th

15 i Our God eternal, reigning

INNSBRUCK

1. Our God e - ter - nal, reign - ing, cre - a - tion's life sus - tain - ing, our ref - uge and_ our_ home; en - throned, in light_ sur - round - ed, when earth was yet_ un - found - ed, the liv - ing God, to him we come.

Music: Traditional song set by Heinrich Isaac (c. 1450–1527)
harmonized by Johann Sebastian Bach (1684–1750)

PSALM 90

The living God 'our refuge and our home'

OUR GOD eternal, reigning,
creation's life sustaining,
　　our refuge and our home;
enthroned, in light surrounded,
when earth was yet unfounded,
　　the living God, to him we come.

2　We fade, a dream that passes,
like withered meadow grasses
　　when summer's sun has shone.
Before that face all-seeing
of God who gave us being
　　we pass away and we are gone.

3　O God of mercy, hear us,
in steadfast love draw near us,
　　from age to age the same;
that we, by grace defended,
when earthly days are ended
　　may live to praise a Saviour's Name.

15 ii Our God eternal, reigning

INNSBRUCK

776 778

1. Our God eternal, reigning, creation's life sus-
tain - ing, our ref - uge and our home; enthroned, in light sur - round - ed, when earth was yet un -
-found - ed, the liv - ing God, to him we come.

Music: Traditional song set by HEINRICH ISAAC (*c.*1450–1527)
Variant of the melody with harmony chiefly based on
JOHANN SEBASTIAN BACH (1684–1750)

PSALM 90

The living God 'our refuge and our home'

OUR GOD eternal, reigning,
creation's life sustaining,
    our refuge and our home;
enthroned, in light surrounded,
when earth was yet unfounded,
    the living God, to him we come.

2   We fade, a dream that passes,
like withered meadow grasses
    when summer's sun has shone.
Before that face all-seeing
of God who gave us being
    we pass away and we are gone.

3   O God of mercy, hear us,
in steadfast love draw near us,
    from age to age the same;
that we, by grace defended,
when earthly days are ended
    may live to praise a Saviour's Name.

16 i Safe in the shadow of the Lord

CREATOR GOD

CM

1. Safe in the sha-dow of the Lord be-neath his hand and power, I trust in him, I trust in him, my fort-ress and my tower.

Music: NORMAN WARREN (*b.* 1934)

PSALM 91

Trust, security and confidence

SAFE in the shadow of the Lord
beneath his hand and power,
    I trust in him,
    I trust in him,
my fortress and my tower.

2   My hope is set on God alone
though Satan spreads his snare;
    I trust in him,
    I trust in him,
to keep me in his care.

4   From fears and phantoms of the night,
from foes about my way,
    I trust in him,
    I trust in him,
by darkness as by day.

5   His holy angels keep my feet
secure from every stone;
    I trust in him,
    I trust in him,
and unafraid go on.

6   Strong in the everlasting Name,
and in my Father's care,
    I trust in him,
    I trust in him,
who hears and answers prayer.

7   Safe in the shadow of the Lord,
possessed by love divine,
    I trust in him,
    I trust in him,
and meet his love with mine.

16 ii Safe in the shadow of the Lord

ABRIDGE (ST STEPHEN)   CM

1. Safe in the sha - dow of the Lord be -
neath his hand and power, I trust in him, I
trust in him, my fort - ress and my tower.

Music: ISAAC SMITH (1734–1805)
   harmonized by EDWARD JOHN HOPKINS (1818–1901)

PSALM 91

Trust, security and confidence

SAFE in the shadow of the Lord
beneath his hand and power,
    I trust in him,
    I trust in him,
my fortress and my tower.

2   My hope is set on God alone
though Satan spreads his snare;
    I trust in him,
    I trust in him,
to keep me in his care.

4   From fears and phantoms of the night,
from foes about my way,
    I trust in him,
    I trust in him,
by darkness as by day.

5   His holy angels keep my feet
secure from every stone;
    I trust in him,
    I trust in him,
and unafraid go on.

6   Strong in the everlasting Name,
and in my Father's care,
    I trust in him,
    I trust in him,
who hears and answers prayer.

7   Safe in the shadow of the Lord,
possessed by love divine,
    I trust in him,
    I trust in him,
and meet his love with mine.

17 i Let this prayer, O Lord, be granted

SHARNBROOK

85 85

1. Let this prayer, O Lord, be grant - ed: may we live and_ grow,_____ fruit - ful trees_____ that God has plant - ed_____ where_____ the_____ wa - ters flow.

Music: PAUL EDWARDS (*b.* 1955)

PSALM 92

Fruitfulness; Scripture; 'the life of heaven'

LET this prayer, O Lord, be granted:
    may we live and grow,
fruitful trees that God has planted
    where the waters flow.

2   When the storms of life assail us
    let our roots be found
firm in hope that will not fail us,
    deep in hallowed ground.

3   Word of God to teach and nourish,
    love of God to tend,
grant us in your courts to flourish,
    fruitful to the end.

4   Then in Christ, our sins forgiven,
    God who loves to bless
call us to the life of heaven,
    trees of righteousness.

17 ii Let this prayer, O Lord, be granted

BODNANT

85 85

1. Let this prayer, O Lord, be grant-ed: may we live and grow, fruit-ful trees that God has plant-ed where the wa - ters flow.

Music: WILLIAM LLEWELLYN (*b.*1925)

PSALM 92

Fruitfulness; Scripture; 'the life of heaven'

LET this prayer, O Lord, be granted:
    may we live and grow,
fruitful trees that God has planted
    where the waters flow.

2   When the storms of life assail us
    let our roots be found
firm in hope that will not fail us,
    deep in hallowed ground.

3   Word of God to teach and nourish,
    love of God to tend,
grant us in your courts to flourish,
    fruitful to the end.

4   Then in Christ, our sins forgiven,
    God who loves to bless
call us to the life of heaven,
    trees of righteousness.

18 The Lord is king, enthroned in might

ELLACOMBE

DCM

1. The Lord is king, en-throned in might on wings of che-ru-bim;
he reigns in ho-li-ness and light, bow down to wor-ship him!
Be-yond all ma-jes-ty and praise his ho-ly Name con-fess:
the King of ev-er-last-ing days, who rules in right-eous-ness.

Music: German Melody, 18th century
as adapted and set in *Gesangbuch*, Mainz, 1833
and harmonized in *Gesangbuch*, St Gallen, 1863
altered by Compilers of *The English Hymnal*, 1906

Psalm 99

The praise of God's holy Name

THE LORD is king, enthroned in might
    on wings of cherubim;
he reigns in holiness and light,
    bow down to worship him!
Beyond all majesty and praise
    his holy Name confess:
the King of everlasting days,
    who rules in righteousness.

2   Of old to priests and prophets known
    with trembling, fear and awe,
he gave his people, set in stone,
    his statutes and his law.
By those who called upon his Name
    the voice of God was heard,
his presence shown in cloud and flame
    when they obeyed his word.

3   O magnify the God of grace
    who hears his people's cry,
and come with songs before his face,
    exalt his Name on high!
to see at last, by grace restored
    from sin and all its stains,
the holy mountain of the Lord
    where God in glory reigns.

Alternative tune: CLAYESMORE

19 To God, our God, the nations' Lord

i

ST FULBERT   CM

1. To God, our God, the nations' Lord, lift ev-ery heart and voice;

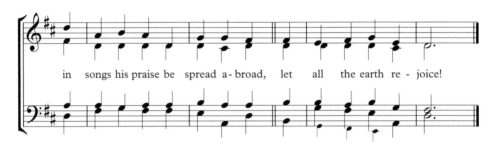

in songs his praise be spread a-broad, let all the earth re-joice!

Music: HENRY JOHN GAUNTLETT (1805–1876)

ii

BROMSGROVE   CM

1. To God, our God, the__ na-tions' Lord, lift__ ev-ery heart and voice;

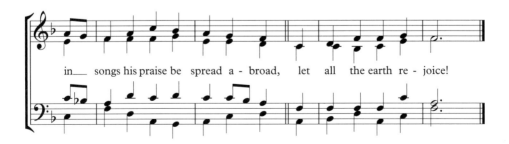

in__ songs his praise be spread a-broad, let all the earth re-joice!

Music: HERBERT ARTHUR DYER (1878–1917)

PSALM 100

Testimony; thankfulness and praise

To GOD, our God, the nations' Lord,
    lift every heart and voice;
in songs his praise be spread abroad,
    let all the earth rejoice!

2   Give thanks to him and bless his Name
        as servants and as friends;
with joy his faithfulness proclaim,
        his love that never ends.

3   For we are his who gave us birth
        and formed us by his will;
the heirs of all his fruitful earth,
        the flock he shepherds still.

4   With thankful hearts then seek his face
        and fill his courts with praise,
our God, of goodness and of grace,
        to everlasting days.

20 Our God be praised, and on his Name be blessing

TORONTO

II 12 13 10

VOICES IN UNISON

1. Our God be praised, and on his Name be bless-ing:____ how rich in
3. May child-ren's child - ren learn that love a - maz - ing,____ all crea-tures

mer - cy to re-deem, how swift to save! He heals and par-dons
bow be-fore his u - ni-ver-sal throne; his whole do-min-ion

those who come their sin con - fess - ing:____
join in e - ver - last - ing____ prais - ing:____

Music: JOHN RUTTER (*b.*1945)

PSALM 103

God's unchanging grace and mercy

praise be to God who res-cues from the grave!
Glo-ry to God, my soul, and God a-lone!

HARMONY

2. High as the hea-vens, see his mer-cy tower-ing! He sets our

sins as far as east is from the west. Our days are brief as

short-lived sum-mer mead-ows' flower-ing,

Dal ℅ for Verse 3

yet in his love we are for e-ver blest.

The unison version for verse 1 may be used for all three verses.

21 Give thanks to God above

i

SM

1. Give thanks to God above and make his

glo - ries known, the Fa - ther whose re -

-deem - ing love still ga - thers in his own.

Music: BENJAMIN MILGROVE (1731–1810)

ii

ST ETHELWALD   SM

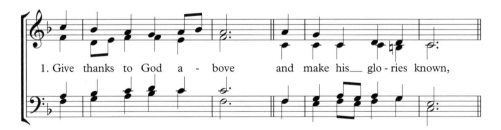

1. Give thanks to God a - bove and make his glo - ries known,

PSALM 107

Human need and divine love

the Fa-ther whose re - deem - ing love still ga - thers in his own.

Music: WILLIAM HENRY MONK (1823–1889)

GIVE THANKS to God above
   and make his glories known,
the Father whose redeeming love
   still gathers in his own.

2   In deserts of despair,
   when faint and far astray,
the Lord himself will meet us there
   and be himself the Way.

3   In darkness and distress,
   and rebels though we be,
he hears us in our helplessness
   and sets the prisoner free.

4   In weight of sin laid low,
   by sickness sore oppressed,
the weary still his welcome know,
   and taste his promised rest.

5   In storm, and tempest-tossed,
   when waves as mountains come,
he stills the seas and leads the lost
   to haven and to home.

6   All things are in his hand:
   rejoice in him who reigns!
For evermore his mercies stand,
   his steadfast love remains.

Alternative tune: SANDYS

22 Rejoice in God, my heart

TRANSFIGURATION

66 84 D

Music: CHRISTOPHER DEARNLEY (1930–2005)

PSALM 111

Joy in God; 'eternal praise'

trace his glo - ries, O my soul, in earth___ and sky.

REJOICE in God, my heart,
    with all whose voices raise
their thankful songs, and take your part
    in ceaseless praise!
His words and works extol,
    exalt his Name on high,
and trace his glories, O my soul,
    in earth and sky.

2   The splendour of his reign
        in majesty appears,
    whose grace and mercy shall remain
        to endless years.
    Secure in him we stand,
        our God, whose ways are just;
    redeemed by his almighty hand,
        in him we trust.

3   His deeds their Lord proclaim,
        with all created things,
    and from the honour of his Name
        all wisdom springs.
    Come share, my soul, the songs
        celestial voices raise,
    and worship him to whom belongs
        eternal praise!

Alternative tune: LEONI (No. 10 in this book)

23 Not to us be glory given

HYFRYDOL

87 87 D

1. Not to us be glory given but to him who reigns above: Glory to the God of heaven for his faithfulness and love! What though unbelieving voices hear no word and see no sign, still in God my

Music: ROWLAND HUW PRITCHARD (1811–1887)

Psalm 115

'Hope is in the living Lord'

heart_ re - joic - es, work - ing out_ his will di - vine.

Not to us be glory given
    but to him who reigns above:
Glory to the God of heaven
    for his faithfulness and love!
What though unbelieving voices
    hear no word and see no sign,
still in God my heart rejoices,
    working out his will divine.

2   Not what human fingers fashion,
        gold and silver, deaf and blind,
dead to knowledge and compassion,
    having neither heart nor mind,
lifeless gods, yet some adore them,
    nerveless hands and feet of clay;
all become, who bow before them,
    lost indeed and dead as they.

3   Not in them is hope of blessing,
        hope is in the living Lord:
high and low, his Name confessing,
    find in him their shield and sword.
Hope of all whose hearts revere him,
    God of Israel, still the same!
God of Aaron! Those who fear him,
    he remembers them by name.

4   Not the dead, but we the living
        praise the Lord with all our powers;
of his goodness freely giving,
    his is heaven; earth is ours.
Not to us be glory given
    but to him who reigns above:
Glory to the God of heaven
    for his faithfulness and love!

24 i Open our eyes, O Lord, we pray

RICHMOND

CM

1. O - pen our eyes,_ O_ Lord,_ we pray, en - light - en heart_ and mind; that as_ we read_ your_ word_ to - day we may_ its trea - sures find.

Music: Melody by THOMAS HAWEIS (1733–1820)
harmonized by SAMUEL WEBBE, *the elder* (1740–1816)

PSALM 119

God's word and our response

OPEN our eyes, O Lord, we pray,
  enlighten heart and mind;
that as we read your word today
  we may its treasures find.

2 Open our ears that, small and still,
    your voice be clearly heard,
  to guide our steps and cleanse our will
    according to your word.

3 Open our lives to love's embrace,
    our dear redeeming Lord:
  your word of life and truth and grace
    within our souls be stored.

4 Open our lips, O Lord, in praise
    to tell what love imparts:
  the work of grace about our ways,
    your word within our hearts.

24 ii Open our eyes, O Lord, we pray

ASHFORD

CM

1. O-pen our eyes, O Lord, we pray, en - light - en heart and mind; that as we read your word to - day we may its trea - sures find.

Music: ERIC THIMAN (1900–1975)

Psalm 119

God's word and our response

Open our eyes, O Lord, we pray,
    enlighten heart and mind;
that as we read your word today
    we may its treasures find.

2   Open our ears that, small and still,
        your voice be clearly heard,
    to guide our steps and cleanse our will
        according to your word.

3   Open our lives to love's embrace,
        our dear redeeming Lord:
    your word of life and truth and grace
        within our souls be stored.

4   Open our lips, O Lord, in praise
        to tell what love imparts:
    the work of grace about our ways,
        your word within our hearts.

Alternative tune: BEATITUDO

25 i I lift my eyes to the quiet hills

DAVOS

98 97

Music: MICHAEL BAUGHEN (*b.* 1930)

PSALM 121

'Kept by the Father's care'

I LIFT my eyes
to the quiet hills
in the press of a busy day;
    as green hills stand
    in a dusty land
so God is my strength and stay.

2   I lift my eyes
to the quiet hills
to a calm that is mine to share;
    secure and still
    in the Father's will
and kept by the Father's care.

3   I lift my eyes
to the quiet hills
with a prayer as I turn to sleep;
    by day, by night,
    through the dark and light
my Shepherd will guard his sheep.

4   I lift my eyes
to the quiet hills
and my heart to the Father's throne;
    in all my ways
    to the end of days
the Lord will preserve his own.

25 ii I lift my eyes to the quiet hills

SOUTH BARRULE   98 97

Music: HOWARD PRIOR (*b.* 1954)

PSALM 121

'Kept by the Father's care'

I LIFT my eyes
to the quiet hills
in the press of a busy day;
    as green hills stand
    in a dusty land
so God is my strength and stay.

2   I lift my eyes
to the quiet hills
to a calm that is mine to share;
    secure and still
    in the Father's will
and kept by the Father's care.

3   I lift my eyes
to the quiet hills
with a prayer as I turn to sleep;
    by day, by night,
    through the dark and light
my Shepherd will guard his sheep.

4   I lift my eyes
to the quiet hills
and my heart to the Father's throne;
    in all my ways
    to the end of days
the Lord will preserve his own.

26 i From the deep places, hear my cry

BRESLAU

LM

1. From the deep plac-es, hear my cry, those hid-den depths of guilt with-in: O God of mer-cy, God Most High, keep no ac-count of all my sin.

Music: German, 15th century,
  as adapted in *As hymnodus sace*, Leipzig, 1625
  harmonized by FELIX MENDELSSOHN-BARTHOLDY (1809–1847)

PSALM 130

Penitence; 'the dew of blessing'

FROM the deep places, hear my cry,
    those hidden depths of guilt within:
O God of mercy, God Most High,
    keep no account of all my sin.

2   Before your glory none can stand,
    no mortal eye behold your face:
extend to me your kingly hand,
    the sovereign touch of saving grace.

3   O Lord, in whom all needs are met,
    draw near in love to me, I pray,
for on your word my hopes are set,
    as watchmen wait for coming day.

4   As watchmen wait till dawn appears,
    so God's redeeming love is shown;
to shed, unfailing through the years,
    the dew of blessing on his own.

26 ii From the deep places, hear my cry

BOROUGH LIGHTS

LM EXTENDED

Music: RICHARD SIMPKIN (*b.* 1969)

PSALM 130

FROM the deep places, hear my cry,
  those hidden depths of guilt within:
O God of mercy, God Most High,
  keep no account of all my sin.

2 Before your glory none can stand,
    no mortal eye behold your face:
  extend to me your kingly hand,
    the sovereign touch of saving grace.

3 O Lord, in whom all needs are met,
    draw near in love to me, I pray,
  for on your word my hopes are set,
    as watchmen wait for coming day.

4 As watchmen wait till dawn appears,
    so God's redeeming love is shown;
  to shed, unfailing through the years,
    the dew of blessing on his own.

The last line of each verse is repeated.

Alternative tune: SONG 34 (No. 2 in this book)

27 i Bless the Lord as day departs

ASTHALL   78 78

Music: JOHN BARNARD (*b.* 1948)

PSALM 134

Evening; grace, peace and mercy

BLESS the Lord as day departs,
    let your lamps be brightly burning,
lifting holy hands and hearts
    to the Lord till day's returning.

2   As within the darkened shrine,
    faithful to their sacred calling,
sons and priests of Levi's line
    blessed the Lord as night was falling;

3   So may we who watch or rest
    bless the Lord of earth and heaven;
and by him ourselves be blest,
    grace and peace and mercy given.

27 ii Bless the Lord as day departs

LAWTON WOODS

78 78

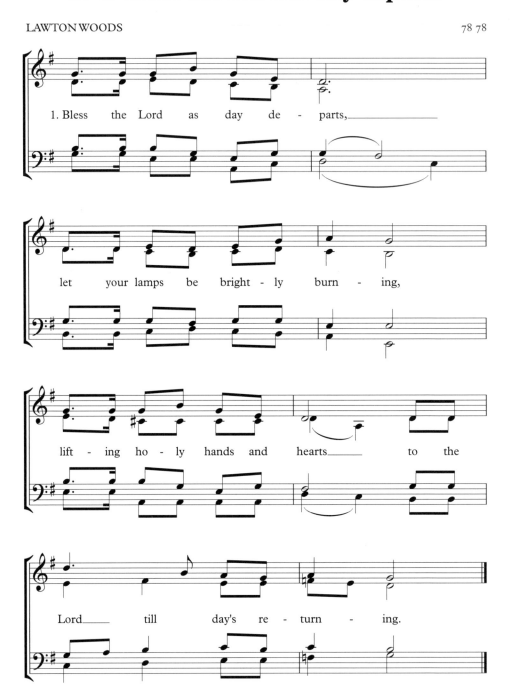

Music: John Carter (*b.* 1930)

PSALM 134

Evening; grace, peace and mercy

BLESS the Lord as day departs,
    let your lamps be brightly burning,
lifting holy hands and hearts
    to the Lord till day's returning.

2   As within the darkened shrine,
    faithful to their sacred calling,
sons and priests of Levi's line
    blessed the Lord as night was falling;

3   So may we who watch or rest
    bless the Lord of earth and heaven;
and by him ourselves be blest,
    grace and peace and mercy given.

28 To God our great salvation

KING'S LYNN

78 78 D

1. To God our great salvation a — tri-umph-song we raise,
with — hymns of a - do - ra - tion and ev-er-last-ing praise.
That — Name be-yond all — nam - ing from age to age a-dored,
we lift on high pro - claim - ing the — great-ness of the Lord.

Music: English folk melody
collected and arranged by RALPH VAUGHAN WILLIAMS (1872–1958)

PSALM 145

Testimony; praise; rejoicing

To GOD our great salvation
    a triumph-song we raise,
with hymns of adoration
    and everlasting praise.
That Name beyond all naming
    from age to age adored,
we lift on high proclaiming
    the greatness of the Lord.

2   Declare in song and story
       the wonders we confess,
who hail the King of Glory
       the Lord our Righteousness.
In loving-kindness caring
       his mercies stand displayed,
forgiving and forbearing
       to all his hand has made.

3   His kingdom knows no ending,
       enthroned in light sublime,
his sovereign power extending
       beyond all space and time.
To us and all things living
       he comes in word and deed,
forbearing and forgiving,
       to meet us in our need.

4   The King of all creation
       is near to those who call;
the God of our salvation
       has stooped to save us all.
Lift high your hearts and voices,
       his praises sound again;
in God his earth rejoices
       for evermore. Amen!

Alternative tune: CRÜGER

29 Praise the God of our salvation

i

MARCHING

87 87

1. Praise the God of our sal-va-tion, all life long your voic-es raise,

stir your hearts to a-dor-a-tion, set your souls to sing his praise!

Music: MARTIN SHAW (1875–1958)

ii

SUSSEX

87 87

1. Praise the God of our sal-va-tion, all life long your voic-es raise,

stir your hearts to a-dor-a-tion, set your souls to sing his praise!

Music: English traditional melody
adapted by RALPH VAUGHAN WILLIAMS (1872–1958)

PSALM 146

'Set your souls to sing his praise'

PRAISE the God of our salvation,
　　all life long your voices raise,
stir your hearts to adoration,
　　set your souls to sing his praise!

2　Turn to him, his help entreating;
　　only in his mercy trust:
human pomp and power are fleeting;
　　mortal flesh is born for dust.

3　Thankful hearts his praise have sounded
　　down the ages long gone by:
happy they whose hopes are founded
　　in the God of earth and sky!

4　Faithful Lord of all things living,
　　by his bounty all are blest;
bread to hungry bodies giving,
　　justice to the long-oppressed.

5　For the strength of our salvation,
　　light and life and length of days,
praise the King of all creation,
　　set your souls to sing his praise!

30 Praise the Lord of heaven

CAMBERWELL

65 65 D

Music: JOHN MICHAEL BRIERLEY (*b.* 1932)

PSALM 148

'Magnify his Name'

PRAISE the Lord of heaven,
　　praise him in the height;
praise him, all his angels,
　　praise him, hosts of light.
Sun and moon together,
　　shining stars aflame,
planets in their courses,
　　magnify his Name!

2　　Earth and ocean praise him;
　　　　mountains, hills and trees;
　　fire and hail and tempest,
　　　　wind and storm and seas.
　　Praise him, fields and forests,
　　　　birds on flashing wings,
　　praise him, beasts and cattle,
　　　　all created things.

3　　Now by prince and people
　　　　let his praise be told;
　　praise him, men and maidens,
　　　　praise him, young and old.
　　He, the Lord of glory!
　　　　We his praise proclaim!
　　High above all heavens
　　　　magnify his Name!

Alternative tune: EVELYNS

INDEX OF TUNES